TROUT FISHING ON
HILL STREAMS

PLATE I

A basket of trout from a hill stream.

TROUT FISHING

ON

HILL STREAMS

By

RICHARD CLAPHAM

OLIVER AND BOYD
EDINBURGH: TWEEDDALE COURT
LONDON: 98 GREAT RUSSELL STREET, W.C.

1947

FIRST PUBLISHED 1947

THIS BOOK IS SET IN 12 POINT PLANTIN

PRINTED IN GREAT BRITAIN BY
A. WALKER AND SON, LTD., GALASHIELS
FOR OLIVER AND BOYD LTD., EDINBURGH

CONTENTS

PHOTOGRAPHS

DRAWINGS

INTRODUCTION

I SERVED my apprenticeship to trout fishing on hill streams. Fifty years ago I killed my first trout on fly in a Yorkshire beck, since when I have fished various fast flowing rocky rivers as far apart as Westmorland and Cornwall, while a sojourn of some years in Northern Ontario afforded me many opportunities to try conclusions with the speckled trout of Canadian waters. During the Great War I carried a few flies with me, and sundry French trout fell for them on various occasions.

Practical experience is the best teacher, and in the following chapters I have endeavoured to set down my opinions for what they are worth. My remarks deal solely with rough rivers, which, being subject to sudden floods, rise and fall quickly. To some, my remarks on trout flies may savour of rank heresy, but the proof of the pudding is in the eating. I have found to my own satisfaction that on rocky, fast-flowing streams the " one-fly man " can easily kill as many or more trout than the angler with the bulging flybook who is for ever changing his feathered lures.

CHAPTER I

THE TROUT

ANGLERS have endowed the trout with many characteristics, chief of which are cunning, and an ability to differentiate between artificial flies and the natural insects they are supposed to represent. Some go so far as to credit it with education. However this may be as regards trout in the slow-flowing streams of the Midlands and the South, it certainly does not apply to the fish of our rough north-country rivers.

Next time you catch a trout cut off the top of its skull. Inside you will find a small cavity, barely half of which is filled by the brain. Scientists tell us that if you remove the brain entirely, the trout can still perform the same actions as a fish that has not been tampered with. Seeing that it is so low in the scale of life, it is difficult to credit the trout with the intelligence that so many people would have us believe. If they said that its behaviour was instinctive, we should be more inclined to agree with them.

EDUCATED TROUT.

There is hardly an angling book to-day, whether dealing with slow-flowing streams or rough rivers, in which the term educated is not applied to the trout. When people speak of an educated fish I take it that they mean one that is difficult to catch, or in other words that it can tell the difference between artificial flies and their natural prototypes. This aptitude is supposedly gained by experience, and the knowledge is then handed down to its descendants. If this be true, the process of education must have been going on since the very earliest fly-fisherman first cast his feathered lure upon the water. We don't know who this angler was, but we do know that in 1496 or thereabouts, " The Boke of Saint Albans " contained a treatise on fly-fishing. If then the education of the trout has been going on for over 400 years, and probably very much longer than that, it is reasonable to suppose that by now the fish should be in the senior wrangler class, able with ease to distinguish counterfeit flies, and thus escape capture altogether. Is this so? Every angler knows the answer.

While we grant that a trout may become temporarily shy through being pricked by a hook, are there not endless instances on record of a fish being caught on the same pattern of fly which had been left in its mouth a short time previously?

HARD FISHED RIVERS.

Again, how about the many free rivers and becks in the North, where, when the water is in condition, you can see numerous artisan and other anglers hard at work with their rods, and all making good baskets. Some of these rivers are extremely hard fished, and if ever trout had a chance to educate themselves, surely it is on these well flogged streams. The trout of these waters are no more difficult to catch to-day than they were generations ago, provided conditions are right. This does not look as if the fish had become educated through experience and heredity. Education has I am afraid nothing to do with it. Every experienced angler knows that there are heavy trout in our rivers and lakes which never rise to flies at all, except possibly in the Mayfly season. These fish, according to the education theorists, should certainly be in the senior wrangler class. Are they? Not a bit of it. Trout above a certain size and weight cease to rise at flies because they prefer more substantial underwater fare like snails, minnows, or members of their own kind. Even in their youth trout are cannibals, and age does not lessen their capacity in this respect.

THE TROUT'S EYESIGHT.

When it comes to eyesight, that of the trout is very acute in low, clear water. One of the first things you learn when serving your apprenticeship to hill-stream fishing is the way in which trout flee at the sight of you when the water is at summer level, unless you tread softly and make an extremely cautious approach from the rear. Rough rivers rise and fall rapidly, and another thing you soon learn is that a rise of water, be

it only a few inches, is sufficient to blunt the
trout's vision, so that in places where you previously had to keep low, you can now stand
upright with impunity.   Should you scare trout
in low water, they will quickly return to their
former position if you stand still.   Sudden
movement alarms them just as it does other
wild creatures, but a stationary object is ignored.
Slow, careful wading upstream will often bring
you very close to trout, and enable you to kill
some of them with a short line and properly
presented fly.

THE TROUT'S HEARING AND SMELLING POWER.

Whether the trout hear as we do, seems to be
a moot point with the scientists.   Every angler
knows that they are peculiarly susceptible to
vibrations, however, and unless you tread softly
on the bank they take warning, and the same
applies when you are wading.   Scientists tell
us that the lateral line on a trout enables it to
detect vibration in the water.   However, this
may be, the cardinal points to remember when
you are after trout are:—keep low and behind
them when the water is at summer level, and make
as little disturbance as possible.   Should the
beck be clearing from a flood there is no need for
subterfuge, and you can walk openly beside the
water as you fish.

Can a trout smell?   It is pretty safe to say
yes!   In my experience when spinning a natural
minnow, it almost invariably kills better than a

PLATE II

Combined "Braemar" type waders.

Devon or other artificial bait of the same size.
The reason for this is I think because the trout
can smell it. That eels can smell is undoubted.
I have more than once watched an eel hunt the
line of a trout which had taken refuge under a
stone. The scent of a fish probably comes down
with the current, just as the " wash " of an otter
does when hounds are hunting it. No doubt
trout can smell worms, as well as that illegal bait,
salmon roe.

CAN A TROUT TASTE?

Can a trout taste its food? I think it is safe to
say yes. At any rate, I have fed a tame trout with
worms which it masticated before swallowing,
which points to the fact that it liked the taste.
Most anglers know how Alfred Ronalds, author
of " The Fly Fisher's Entomology," threw dead
house flies to a trout, some of which were doctored
with cayenne pepper, mustard, oil and vinegar.
All the flies were taken and from the experiment
Ronalds concluded that a trout's palate is not
peculiarly sensitive.

Trout are often credited with fastidiousness
about their food, but after conducting hundreds
of autopsies on hill-stream as well as lake fish,
I have always found that they were decidedly
catholic in this respect. As a rule the stomach
contents consisted of grubs and nymphs, with
occasional specimens of winged insects. Other
creatures which trout have been known to take
include members of their own kind, minnows,

sticklebacks, loach, frogs, worms, maggots, beetles, leeches, slugs, rats, crayfish, snails and young water fowl.

STOMACH CONTENTS.

The most curious stomach contents that I have heard of were given in *The Field* of September 23rd, 1926. They were taken from a 3 lb. 5 oz. trout caught on a Coachman in the Derbyshire Wye, and consisted of worms, snails, half a burnt match-stick, bit of coal $\frac{3}{4}$ inch long, piece of an old paint brush or shaving brush, 2 inches of a rasher of bacon with the rind on, bits of onion, celery stalks or hemlock stalks, and what appeared to be bits of wax candle.

Turning to my own angling diary, I find that a lake trout killed in June on a natural minnow had a stomach full of Black Gnats and Stonefly grubs. Another lake trout of $13\frac{3}{4}$ oz. also taken on natural minnow, was full of fresh-water snails, and a third weighing 1 lb. $9\frac{1}{4}$ oz. was likewise crammed with snails. A reservoir trout which took a natural minnow had fed greedily on caddis grubs and snails, while nine other trout from the same water were full of caddis, minnows, and a few winged flies. Three trout taken on fly in April from a hill stream had fed on caddis grubs. In the stomach of one fish were three pebbles. Twenty trout taken on fly in June from another hill-stream had eaten small green caterpillars, creepers, and stoneflies, plus Bracken Clock Beetles, and various other grubs and insects.

PLATE III

The bridge pool on the Troutbeck.

From the foregoing it will be seen that trout from rough rivers feed chiefly on subaquatic creatures, and only occasionally take winged insects from the surface.

SLIMLY BUILT FLIES.

On a hill-stream, moorland beck, or any rapid river, trout have little or no time in which to pick and choose their food. Underwater fare swept down by the current is instantly seized or missed. For this reason one or two patterns of artificial flies are quite sufficient when you are fishing a beck. Provided your flies are slimly built and reasonable in size they will give an impressionistic idea of living insects, and that is all you require in fast water. Now and then a trout may intercept a fully matured fly on the surface, but for one such it will take a hundred subaqueous tit-bits. Thus, to tie your flies in imitation of particular insects is sheer waste of time. Nor is the colour of your flies important. When it comes to recognition of colour, experiments seem to prove that the trout's sense in this respect is less acute than our own. Personally when fishing rough rivers I don't worry about the colour of my flies. My favourite fly is the Black Spinner better known in the North as Lee's Favourite. It is dressed as follows:—Tail, two fibres of black cock's hackle. Body—black silk ribbed with silver. Hackle—black. Wings—snipe or starling. The tail is an unnecessary appendage as it kills quite as well without.

B

Strictly speaking black is not a colour, but I have always found a black fly very killing when conditions are right. The subject of trout flies is dealt with in another chapter.

We all know that trout exhibit wonderful agility. They can also fight and do so during the spawning season when duels take place for possession of the females. They use their teeth just like a dog or a fox. A trout that is in possession of a good feeding station may be driven off by a larger and heavier fish that takes its place.

FISHING AT NIGHT.

If you fish at night you will find that the trout are chiefly on the shallows. As dusk falls big moths and other insects make their appearance, and the trout are ready for them. The usual practice when fishing at night is to use a brown, yellow or white moth attached to strong gut. This in the north is known as " bustard fishing." The yellow and white moths are favourite lures, as they are supposed to show up better in the darkness. There is a fallacy about this, however. The scientists' definition of colour is light distributed amongst particles of matter, thus when the light goes there can be no colour, and a black fly will be seen as readily as a white one. Trout often feed greedily at night, and heavy baskets are frequently made.

COLOUR OF TROUT.

Every angler knows how trout in a stream vary in colour. Here is one of an almost golden shade, there another nearly black. The protective colouring of trout to match their surroundings is affected, so the scientists tell us—by visual impression, so that the pigment cells change their form. Apparently the black trout are those suffering from blindness in one or both eyes, or from the attacks of internal parasites.

The question sometimes arises, is trout fishing cruel? A trout contains blood, and often feels distinctly warm when taken out of the net. Against that all the evidence goes to show that it has practically no sense of feeling or pain. I have on a number of occasions captured trout on whose bodies were the healed scars of what had evidently been desperate wounds, wounds so severe that only a nerveless creature could possibly have survived them. Most experienced anglers can bring forward similar evidence.

In order to show how little the stomach of a trout is influenced by foreign matter, I quote the case of a quarter-pounder which had swallowed a large bait hook and a length of strong gut, part of which was protruding from its mouth. I hooked this trout on fly in a hill-stream, and it fought with the usual dash of its kind. When brought to net it was in very good condition. Many such incidents go to prove that a wound that would be undoubtedly fatal to a higher animal is of no moment whatever to a trout.

WHERE TROUT LIE.

In winter if you peer into the water from the parapet of a bridge not a sign of a trout is to be seen. Look again when the spring has advanced, say in April, and you will find that the fish have left their winter quarters and are lying in full view. Many of them will be small, but here and there you will see a good trout awaiting what the current brings down in the way of food. At first, when out of condition the fish inhabit slack water, but as their condition improves, they move up into the rapids. Where the current is strong they do not buck the full force of the water while occupying their favourite hovers, because the latter afford shelter. A trout will lie behind a rock or big stone, or he may occupy a depression in the river-bed where the water is practically still. From such a hover he will dart into the current to seize food that is being swept down. He has no time to pick and choose, and for this reason, as already mentioned, the pattern of fly you offer him matters not at all, provided it gives an impressionistic idea of a living insect.

WHEN A FLOOD COMES.

From May to August the trout are in tip-top condition, after which they fall off as the spawning season approaches. Fly-fishing upstream when the water is at summer level generally means that you hook a larger percentage of small trout than good ones, but should a flood come down, the big trout leave their hiding places and you stand a good chance of killing them. At first the water is thick and a well scoured worm proves a deadly bait. After a time the stream begins to clear, and you can then fish minnow or fly, whichever you prefer. The minnow generally kills well when the water is beginning to rise. The coming flood tempts the larger fish to leave their low water retreats and visit the tails of streams and other places.

TROUT FOOD.

The chief trout food in a rough water consists of the larvae of aquatic insects. One of the most useful items on the menu is caddis, as it is about the only thing that can withstand the grinding action of the winter floods. Much of the insect larvae first appears in wet and marshy places adjacent to the beck, where watercress, marsh marigolds, etc., grow. Such food gradually seeps its way to the main stream. Water moss, which grows on rocks and bouldrs is about the only plant capable of weathering the action of floods. It, too, provides its quota of trout food. Probably the most valuable food, owing to its size, is the stone-fly and its larva, the " creeper."

IMPROVING THE BECK.

When considering the food supply of a rocky river, one must remember that such a stream is subject to sudden floods. This means that while to-day and to-morrow the entire bed of the beck may be submerged, there shortly follows a rapid fall until eventually a great portion of the river bottom becomes exposed and dry. Such exposed portions are useless as breeding grounds for aquatic insects. It can therefore be understood that the majority of insect food in the way of larvae is produced in wet ground adjacent to the beck and not in the beck itself. It is not a difficult matter, however, to improve the breeding conditions in the river if you are prepared to face a certain amount of hard work in the construction of rough stone dams which will form pools, and so keep valuable areas of gravel permanently under water. Such pools quickly form larders in which the trout foregather, and add greatly to your sport when fly-fishing. The subject of improving the food supply of rough rivers will be further discussed in a later chapter.

The novice who is starting his trout fishing career on the becks may have been led to believe that he is up against a peculiarly well educated and wily quarry. Let him take heart, however, for he will find that in this respect the trout has been overrated. With experience he will discover that atmospherical conditions play a much greater part than a well stocked fly-book when it comes to filling a creel.

CHAPTER II

TROUT FLIES

FIFTY years ago I was first shown how to throw a fly. My mentor lived in a little Yorkshire village, and what he didn't know about filling a creel was hardly worth knowing. He tied his own flies, and used horse-hair casts. A very few patterns of flies sufficed him, all of which were very lightly tied. They included Snipe and Purple, Dotterel and Orange, and the Waterhen Bloa known in the vernacular as " t'watterhen."

Like other youthful fishermen I gradually accumulated a collection of flies with which I rang the changes. Then I was given a copy of Stewart's " Practical Angler," and found that he —like my old Yorkshire friend—pinned his faith to half a dozen patterns, all of which were lightly dressed. His favourite was the Black Spider. One day when spring-cleaning my fly-book preparatory to the coming season, the sight of so many different patterns set me wondering whether I needed them all. If half a dozen patterns were enough for a practical fisherman like Stewart or my village teacher, why could not the list be still further reduced? From that moment I decided to choose a couple of patterns and fish them for a season in order to compare the total catch with those of previous seasons. The two flies I selected for the test were the Black Spider, and the Black Spinner, the dressing of which is given in the previous chapter.

The Black Spinner is a lightly dressed winged fly, and it had on many occasions proved its worth. The Black Spider is dressed with the small feather of a cock starling and brown silk.

CONFIDENCE AND TWO PATTERNS.

Believe me it took some strength of mind to break away from my old change-fly habit, but I did it, and I very soon began to have absolute confidence in my two chosen patterns. Here, let me tell you, confidence in your feathered lures is more than half the battle when fly-fishing. At the end of my first trial season I found I had killed more trout with my two flies than had fallen to my rod in previous seasons. That was good enough for me. Thenceforward I used nothing but these two flies. To-day, more often than not the Black Spinner is the only pattern on my cast, thus I am practically a one-fly man.

The success of my two flies can be attributed I think to the fact that I kept them in the water, and no time was wasted in changing from one pattern to another as was my former habit. I am one of those who go fishing to catch fish, and I find that the less time I waste the heavier my creel is likely to be at the end of the day.

handle big fish, and not too thick for use in clear water.   It is a mistake to use ultra fine gut.

Confidence.

As previously mentioned, confidence in your fly or flies is half the battle.   Once you have gained this confidence, you fish them as they should be fished and keep them in the water where they belong.   Changing flies only wastes time, yet the average angler constantly does it. On a day when trout are reluctant to rise he goes through his whole gamut of patterns and should he finally begin to take fish he says to himself " it was that last change that did the trick." Poor fellow.   If the trout begin to take really well he will find that a return to the fly he started with will provide just as much sport as the last. But, and it is a big but, it requires some strength of mind to do so.

Presentation.

Unfortunately for most anglers a brief yearly holiday of a fortnight does not afford sufficient time in which to test theories.   You need to fish your flies throughout a season or seasons, and in all sorts of atmospherical conditions. While a trout or two are always possible it is only on the few and far between red letter days when atmospherical conditions are in your favour that you can fill your creel to overflowing.   Unless these conditions are favourable, no amount of changing will improve your sport.   Given you have confidence in your flies, success with them depends to a great extent on the manner in which you present them to the trout.   With some people this is a gift, just as " hands " are with some horsemen.   The art of presentation can be acquired by practice, and it is well worth culti-vating.   Success depends on " the man behind the rod."   Just as some men have " hands," others have an instinctive knowledge of the places where trout are likely to be found when " fishing the water."   Even on a strange river such people are seldom at a loss.

Crude as our artificial flies are in comparison with the natural insects, trout take them so well at times that one wonders why the red-letter days are so infrequent.   It cannot be the fault of the flies.   Was every fishing day a red-letter one, however, we should soon tire of angling because the uncertainty would be eliminated, and it is just this uncertainty that makes the sport so attractive.

NYMPHS AND LARVÆ.

As mentioned in a previous chapter, the chief food of the trout consists of subaquatic creatures such as larvae and nymphs, fully fledged insects being only occasional items on the menu.   It is logical therefore in most instances to offer them such flies.   The majority of standard artificials are winged, because they were originally so tied under the supposition that they represented fully fledged insects which had been blown on to the water and there drowned. Later it of course became known that river insects are hatched from eggs laid beneath the surface and that before they become fully matured they rise from the bottom as nymphs, during which period the trout take them under water. It is quite safe to say that most, if not all of our lightly tied flies both winged and hackled, must represent nymphs in the eyes of the trout when such artificials are fished wet.

On Striking.

Nymph fishing, as such, is now part and parcel of dry fly fishing on the Midland and Southern streams. The method is to cast an artificial nymph either upstream or up and across to a trout that is feeding. The nymph is of course fished wet, but the gut is often greased to within a foot or two of the fly so that it floats, the idea being that when a trout takes, the floating gut is drawn under and so gives notice of the fact. When fishing a cast of wet flies in fast water you get no such plain notice. Perhaps you glimpse movement in the neighbourhood of your flies, or a faint gleam under water may warn you. Even after years of wet fly fishing I find it difficult to explain just how one knows when to tighten. It is really a sort of instinct. Many trout in fast water hook themselves, especially when you are fishing down-stream. The difference between fishing a floating fly and a team of wet flies lies in the fact that with the former you see all that goes on, whereas with the latter you need both a quick eye and a certain amount of intuition. You can of course use a floating fly on a rough hill stream should you so desire or you can employ a team of flies with one wet and two dry, or two wet and one dry. On many a day when trout are taking wet flies really well, however, you may see few if any rise to surface food, and on the whole I have always found that wet flies kill much the best.

The Bracken Clock Beetle.

There is one exception and that is when trout are taking Bracken Clock beetles. In June these beetles often swarm amongst the fern, and many of them find their way into the water. When this happens you can fish the natural beetle, or the floating artificial known as "Kennedy's Beetle." Using the latter I have had some very good baskets on the becks. I shall have something to say about natural trout baits in a later chapter.

" Fine and as near as you can."

In most angling books you are advised to fish " fine and far off " but in practice you will find it better to change this to " fine and as near as you can." For beck fishing, even in low water, 3x gut, as already mentioned, is quite fine enough. New, sound gut will lift a surprising weight. You can, for example, raise 3 lb. with a 3x cast. This means that when you hook

PLATE IV

Netting a trout on a Yorkshire beck.

a decent trout you can hold him and hustle him to the net without waste of time. Many anglers are afraid to trust their gut and put on pressure, and they let a fish play about when they could easily hold it. Sound 3x gut, and a fly tied on a No. 2 hook that takes a good bite will hold anything in reason. On a red letter day time is precious, and you can't afford to waste it by using ultra fine tackle and letting your fish fool about.

A SHORT LINE.

By using as short a line as possible you have instant control over a hooked fish and can at once hustle him downstream. This is important in low, clear water so as not to create more disturbance than necessary. Other trout may lie just ahead, and the antics of a hooked fish soon alarm them unless you pull it down in a hurry. In a biggish fly-water when good trout are lying in a strong current, you can often use a surprisingly short line if you are casting upstream with a fairly long rod. Quite recently I fished down a fast stream twice without a touch. Then, wading close to the bank, I fished it up. The travel of the flies was very short, but I killed six trout just under half a pound apiece, and lost two others. Many times a trout rose and missed owing to the speed and roughness of the current, but the capture of the half-dozen made quite an exciting bit of fishing. While a dainty 7 ft. fly-rod is very nice to handle, its shortness handicaps you when making a close approach, as you have to use a longer line than with a lengthier rod. The longer the line you use in fast water when fishing up, the less control you have over it, and control in this case is most important. There are times and places of course where you must use a long line, but the nearer you can get the better.

FLASHING FLIES.

Many trout flies, especially those dressed with silver or gold bodies, exhibit a surprising amount of flash when the light strikes them. Even without metallic dressing the feathers of many flies still show this flash. Such flies are no doubt taken for small fish, because the latter flash when they turn and are on an uneven keel. A biggish silver-bodied fly drawn upstream in short jerks often kills quite as well as a spinning bait.

I have seen artificial flies into the making of which an extraordinary amount of work had been put. These flies were constructed of various iridescent material which gave them a most realistic appearance in the hand, whereas in the water there was a different tale to tell. There they were dead and lifeless, being too stiff to show attractive movement. Beautiful as these artificials were to look at, a simply tied hackle fly licked them hollow when it came to killing trout.

RED-LETTER DAYS.

If you are one of those who have had the luck to fish right through the season for a number of

years, you will know that from time to time
between April and the end of September, there
are certain red-letter days on which the trout
take so well that it is an easy matter to fill your
creel. Should you have kept a fishing diary
turn back its pages, and you will find that those
red-letter days were few and far between. Let
me give you a few instances from my own
diary.

In 1913 I opened the season on March 5th
with 5 trout. Between then and April 9th I
had eight days fishing, and the total ranged from
6 to 32 trout. On April 14th I had a good day
and killed 40 nice fish. Four moderate days
followed, and then on April 25th I creeled 41
trout. April 29th was not a bad day, total
34 trout. Until May 7th there was not much
doing, but on that date I killed 51 trout. After
that I had nineteen poor and moderate days,
until on June 11th a basket of 57 trout was
accounted for. From June 12th to 17th I was
out on four days, and the totals varied from
4 trout to 20 trout. Then on June 27th I had
four days fishing, best day 28 trout, worst day
15 trout. On June 30th I had 52 trout. Between
then and July 3rd I was not out, but on the latter
date I killed 61 trout. From then till July 15th
I had five days fishing, best day 26 trout, worst
day 3 trout. On July 18th 41 trout came to hand.
The following day I got 19 trout. Then followed nine days on which the total varied from
6 trout to 38 trout. September 27th—my best

day—gave 17 fish. During the entire season there were only eight really good days, when baskets of 40, 51, 51, 57, 86, 52, 61 and 41 trout were killed. The diary records better seasons as well as worse than the above, but it serves to show that the red-letter days are infrequent.

Atmospherical Conditions.

The question arises, why, if the trout responded so well on eight days, did they not repeat the performance every day? The same flies were used on each occasion. They could not have been hungry on those particular days only. As a matter of fact every fish killed was crammed with grubs and other sub-aquatic items. It was not hunger therefore which brought them to my flies, for they kept on taking avidly despite the fact that they were full to overflowing. No, we can set aside the hunger theory, for hunger alone will not cause trout to all rise simultaneously. We must turn, I think, to atmospherical conditions if we are to find an answer to the question. There is a condition of the atmosphere that on the majority of days keeps the trout down. Was it possible to undo the influence of this condition so that the trout would rise all day and every day, the uncertainty of the sport would be gone, and our interest in fishing would quickly evaporate. Not only that, we should take such a heavy toll of the trout that their ranks would be unduly thinned, in fact they would be in danger of extermination.

Is it not possible, in fact most probable, that Providence takes a hand in these matters, and so arranges things that the trout are saved from their own greed, while we retain our interest in fishing because a measure of uncertainty is provided that keeps us plugging away in hopes that sport will improve.

CHAPTER III

NORTH-COUNTRY FLY PATTERNS

IF you delve into the history of north-country wet fly patterns, you will discover that little or no entomological knowledge was possessed by the anglers who first tied them. Any scraps of material their inventors had on hand went into the making of the slim-built winged and hackled lures which still kill as well as ever they did on our hill-streams and becks. Christened after the silk and feather of which they were made, these flies give an impressionistic idea of insects in general, and they kill because the movements of their soft feathers in fast water suggest life. That they should kill was all that mattered to the men who first tied them.

How they got their Names.

There is a long list of these north-country flies, amongst which are the Dotterel and Orange, Woodcock and Orange, Orange Partridge, Golden Plover and Yellow, Snipe and Purple, Black Spider, Grouse and Orange, Hare's Lug, Waterhen Bloa, Dark Watchett, etc. Although the majority are christened after their tying materials, others took the names of their inventors, such as Lee's Favourite, Greenwell's

Glory, John Spencer, Bousfield's Fancy, Ramsbottom's Favourite, and Broughton Point. The last mentioned was first tied by old Jack Broughton, in his day a celebrated Eden fisherman. Ramsbottom's Favourite was invented by Mr R. Ramsbottom of Clitheroe, who was well known on the Ribble.

In some cases the nomenclature of these flies, such as Waterhen Bloa, and Dark Watchett, may puzzle the Southerner. The term bloa coincides with the Scottish blae, and the Westmorland and Cumberland blea. There is for example the Black and Blae trout fly, and that moorland plant the blaeberry or bilberry, while in Lakeland you have Blea Tarn. The dictionary definition of the word blae signifies blackish or blue in colour: livid: bleak. (Middle English, blo, bloo—Scandinavian, bla).

The word watchett is spelt watchet in the dictionary, and the meaning is given as pale-blue (Middle English, wachet, perhaps connected with woad). A Dark Watchett trout fly is the shade of the Iron Blue Dun. It is a hackled pattern.

LOCAL FEATHERS FOR FLIES.

North-country fly-tiers found all they wanted in the way of feathers amongst the game and other birds of their own localities. Grouse, partridge, snipe, woodcock, golden plover, waterhen, starling, etc., all provided their quota, as well as the far-famed dotterel, a bird once plentiful on the Yorkshire and Lakeland fells, but now practically extinct as a breeding species south of the Border. It was owing to the extraordinary demand for dotterel feathers for fly-tying that the birds were gradually reduced in numbers. They were exceedingly tame and an easy mark for the shooter. In Cumberland the Dotterel Dun is a favourite trout fly. The old dressing is as follows:—Body—brown fur from a hare's face. Hackle—a feather from the outside of the dotterel's wing. In the modern dressing a feather from the inside of a starling's wing replaces that from a dotterel. The Yorkshire dressing of this fly has an orange silk body instead of the hare's fur. To-day the dotterel no longer breeds in Lakeland, but a few pairs still manage to carry out their family affairs on the Grampian mountains in Scotland despite the ceaseless forays of the egg-collecting fraternity.

FLIES TAKEN FOR NYMPHS.

As mentioned in a previous chapter, it is quite safe to assert that these lightly tied north-country flies both winged and hackled, are taken by the trout for nymphs. The latter are the pupæ of the Ephemeridæ. Some live under stones, some in the mud, and others amongst weeds. Sooner or later they have to ascend to the surface where they hatch out, and it is chiefly during this ascent that the trout intercept them. It is the swimming larvæ that live amongst the weeds, and trout will rout amongst the latter to find them, as well as take them during their upward journey. Attempts have been made by those who fish the slow flowing rivers of the Midlands and the South, to imitate nymphs. I have seen some of these imitations, and very dead looking things they were. Out of curiosity I tried them on the becks, but quickly found that a lightly dressed hackle or spider fly licked them hollow. They failed to afford that flicker in the current provided by the soft feather of the north-country patterns. Nymphs are for the most part lively creatures and show a certain amount of " flash," thus a lightly dressed winged fly with silver ribbing, such as the Black Spinner, kills well when fished wet, because it doubtless affords an impressionistic idea of a nymph. When atmospherical conditions are right, a state of affairs that only occurs at tantalizingly long intervals, any of the slimly built north-country trout flies will fill a creel. Open the fish you catch, and you will find them crammed with nymphs, which points strongly to the fact that your sunken flies are taken by the trout for these pupæ.

HORSEHAIR FOR CASTS.

In the old days, and to a certain extent even now, our north-country flies were tied to horsehair. The advantages of horsehair are that it is far more durable than gut, and it possesses a considerable amount of elasticity. You can immerse it in water for any length of time without

injuring its usefulness, and it does not fray like
gut should it come in contact with stones or
other objects.   Even when soaked it still retains a
certain amount of " life," and thus seldom gets
tangled up.   Should it do so, a little shaking
will generally overcome the trouble.   One of its
great advantages is that dropper flies tied on it
stand out clear of the main cast and are less likely
to catch up in the latter than when using gut.

The disadvantages of hair are that once it has
been stretched to the limit it becomes brittle and
useless, and even the best of hair is much inferior
to good gut as regards strength.   Nor can a hair
cast be driven so far against the wind as one
composed of gut.   If hair possessed the strength
of gut it would be almost perfect for angling use.
Hair is also supposed to be less visible than gut.

Picking your Fishing Days.

North-country anglers who live practically
beside their rivers and becks pick their fishing
days.   When flood water begins to come down,
most of them can be seen digging worms, or seeing
to those which they already have scouring in
moss.   Then, when the beck is up and the water
thick, they set to work.   Until the water begins
to clear they fish worm, after which they turn
their attention to downstream fly-fishing.   Even
yet some of the older village anglers make their
own rods, or get the carpenter to do it for them.
These weapons are usually long and pliant, just
the thing for down-stream work with hair casts.

In the old days, owing to less efficient drainage, it took the water a considerable time to run down, whereas now the process is much quicker, so that ideal fishing conditions are considerably shorter than they used to be. The old-timers caught some wonderful baskets of trout. They were the envy of my youthful existence, until my father fitted me out with a rod and tackle, and placed me in the hands of one of them, who soon taught me the rudiments of the sport.

THE YOUNGER GENERATION.

Since then a younger generation of anglers has sprung up. A generation who use split bamboo rods, and can fish the wet fly up-stream with any one. Amongst them is my good friend, the postman, who, during his off-duty hours, spends much time beside the beck from whence he seldom returns without a worth-while basket. These men still use the flies that were favoured by their ancestors, and their entomological knowledge is nothing to write home about. As long as their flies kill they are perfectly satisfied, and care not at all whether they are supposed to represent natural insects.

When you come to think of it, the science of fly-tying has really advanced very little, if at all, when it comes to the actual killing of trout. Certainly many new patterns of flies have been produced, but they kill no better, if as well, as the softly hackled, impressionistic types which have been used from very early times.

PRACTICE AND THEORY.

For some anglers there are two sides to fishing, the practical and the theoretical. One man may theorize and attempt to explore the mysteries of underwater vision and the like, while another goes out to fill a basket if he can, and cares not two hoots what his flies represent as long as they kill. One has read of an angler discontinuing the use of a certain pattern of fly—despite the fact that it was a good all round the season killer—simply because he could not make up his mind which particular natural insect it represented. After all, a fly that in our eyes looks as perfect an imitation of a particular insect as human hands can make it, may appear as something quite different in the eyes of a trout, provided the latter has time to examine it. They tell us that when the trout of the slow flowing southern rivers are feeding on the natural olive duns, that a gold-ribbed Hare's Ear often kills very well. Now an olive dun is smooth-bodied and olive green, while the above mentioned fly is greyish-brown, with a rough body ribbed with gold. In the hand, the natural insect and the artificial are as unlike in appearance as chalk and cheese, yet the trout take the fly freely when the olive duns are about, thus the artificial that looks nothing like a dun in our eyes may be so suggestive of one from the trout's point of view that the fish unhesitatingly accepts it. Until we see with the eyes of a trout from a trout's environment, we cannot tell for certain what either the natural

insect or the artificial fly actually looks like.
For most of us life is too short to delve into the
scientific side of angling, and even if we did so,
should we be any wiser, or would our sport
improve! I doubt it! Certainly on our fast
running rivers and becks there is no need to worry
your head about the fly question. To the trout
lying in a rapid current it is a case of " That's
food—that was." He must dash at the sunken
nymph or the surface fly without hesitation, for
he has no time to examine it. Thus the artificial that suggests life and affords an impressionistic idea of an insect is all you require when out
to make a basket of fish on the becks.

OLD TIMERS AND OLD DAYS.

In my youth, nearly all the old-timers tied
their own flies. The latter might look a bit
rough compared with the professionally tied
article of to-day, but they killed to some tune
when conditions were right. In these days of
intensive advertising the village anglers generally send away for their flies, although now and
then you meet a man who is nimble with his
fingers at blending an attraction of silk and
feathers. When it comes to fishing on the hill
streams, it is not always the angler with the up-
to-date outfit who kills the most trout. Many a
countryman takes very little care of his rod, and
you may see it leant carelessly against his cottage
porch, or laid across a row of nails on a beam.
The visiting angler may be inclined to scoff when

he sees it, but probably before his holiday is over he will have had good cause to envy both it and its owner should the nearby river have been in fishing order. In the old days when wages were low, many a working man in the northern villages made quite a bit of pocket money by the sale of trout. He could be pretty sure of getting rid of his catch if he took it up to the Big House, with usually a pint of home-brewed ale into the bargain. To-day the old Hall is probably occupied by strangers, or has been turned into an hotel. The beck is still there, but one doesn't seem to hear of the heavy baskets that used to be made by the old-timers. Autres temps, autres moeurs, more's the pity.

CHAPTER IV

SPINNING FOR TROUT

SPINNING for trout often affords very good sport on a rough river. When the latter is in normal flow you can practice the upstream method, but your best chance of filling a creel is to spin downstream when the water is clearing after a flood. Trout also take the minnow well in a rising water before it gets too thick.

For occasional spinning on a small stream you can use a stiffish fly-rod and ordinary reel. Strip off a yard or two of line and " shoot " it as the bait goes out. To retrieve it, pull in line by hand, or, if your reel is pretty full of line, wind up quickly in the ordinary way. I have killed both brown trout and mignatory fish in this manner, but it does not of course compare with a proper spinning outfit.

SPECIAL ROD AND REEL.

Really to enjoy spinning you require a special rod and reel. On the average hill stream a 7 ft. or 8 ft. rod is suitable. For preference it should be built of split bamboo. The reel may be of the revolving type, or a fixed spool. If you use a free-running reel you must brake with your finger when the bait enters the water, otherwise you will get an overrun that results in a horrible " bird's nest." There is a decided knack, which many people never seem to learn, in managing such a reel so as to avoid overruns, and for this reason the average angler will be best suited with a reel that is mechanically controlled, such as Allcock's " Easicast," or a good English-made multiplier like Hardy's " Elarex." Of fixed spool reels there are a number of patterns, including the "Altex," "Illingworth," " Magnacast," etc. With a fixed spool reel it is impossible to get an overrun. Gut substitute forms the best line for such a reel, whereas a dressed or undressed silk line is suitable for the revolving drum type.

BRAIDED NYLON LINE.

Since writing the above, Mr L. R. Hardy, of Hardy Brothers, the well known tackle firm, very kindly sent me one of the new, braided Nylon spinning lines to try. This line has a breaking strain of 8.5 lbs., and has been double treated. It is off-white in colour, and looks like silk. So far I have fished this line for 20 hours, and have killed a number of sea trout with it. It casts beautifully from a fixed spool reel, because there is a minimum of coil friction and lip friction over the drum. The line is very round and smooth, and being waterproof it floats until the weight of the bait pulls it under. With this line I can cast further than with a gut substitute-line. While I have not so far used this

PLATE V

Up-stream fly-fishing near the head of a Lakeland beck.

line for a long enough period to test it for wear and tear, or its reaction to a heavy fish, other users who have been able to test the material say that its wearing qualities are far ahead of gut substitute. My experience leads me to believe that braided Nylon makes the best spinning line so far produced, and there is little doubt that this material will become extremely popular after the war. Mr L. R. Hardy is the pioneer of these lines. He began using them eight years ago, and in conjunction with the Nylon makers all the initial troubles were overcome, and now their efforts have been rewarded by the production of an ideal spinning line. Owing to the war, Nylon lines are not in regular production, those in existence having been made for experimental purposes only. In peace time they will be on the market. These lines are made in this country from Dupont, I.C.I. and Canadian Nylon Yarn.

SPINNING BAITS

Of spinning baits we have the natural and artificial. You can get the latter in all sizes, shapes and materials. Many of them are most artistically painted in representation of various fish. Attractive as these painted baits look to the angler who is buying them from a eulogistic tackle maker, the careful work upon them is utterly wasted for when a bait spins all the coloured markings merge, and the lure becomes uniform in shade. On the whole a small silver

Devon from an inch to an inch and a half in length is as good as anything. A quill minnow is also very killing. Using the $1\frac{1}{4}$ inch size, I have made some heavy baskets on the becks. Even in fast water where any bait will spin, it is advisable to use one with large enough fins so as to ensure that when it leaves the current for the slacker water near the side it will continue to spin properly. Trout have a habit of seizing a bait as it leaves the current, and if at that moment it slows down the fish sheers off. When using a spinning bait change it every half hour or so for another with reverse spin in order to avoid line twist. Two swivels on a trace are quite sufficient. Various patterns of anti-kink gadgets can be attached to the trace ostensibly to counteract twist, but in practice it is better to rely on changing the bait, for the less you have on the trace in the way of such anti-kink devices the better. In the same way with a lead, the weight should be in the bait itself and not on the trace. This enables you to cast far more accurately than when a light bait is flying loose beyond the lead. Another thing: a lead on the trace only serves to distract attention from the bait. I have known both brown trout and mignatory fish to run at a lead. When spinning for sea trout you can, if you like, use a dropper fly above the bait. I have often thought that when a fish takes this fly it does so because it imagines the bait is chasing the feathered lure, and so the fish dashes in and seizes it out of jealousy.

Artificial v. Natural Bait.

We may now ask, does an artificial spinning bait kill as well as a natural bait! Speaking from my own experience I say no, although there may not be a great deal in it on a good day when trout are taking the minnow eagerly. There are various tackles for natural minnow such as the " Archer," etc., but the one I like best is the celluloid scarab because it gives perfect protection to the bait, and being transparent, enables the minnow to be easily seen. Enclosed in scarabs, a couple of reverse spin minnows will last for several days spinning if need be, and I have known them to kill when they had almost reached the mummy stage.

If you live where minnows are plentiful, fresh ones can be used, otherwise preserved ones will do quite well. A formalin solution to which a few drops of glycerine have been added makes a good preservative. Before placing a minnow in a scarab, cut off all the fins except the tail. Choose minnows that are a good fit in the scarab, neither too big nor too small. If you err at all let it be on the small side. A bait from $1\frac{1}{4}$ in. to $1\frac{1}{2}$ in. long is about right.

Baits and Flash.

Why do spinning baits kill? The answer seems to be because they flash. If you are fishing with live bait you will notice that the latter flashes in its efforts to escape. For this reason when putting a minnow into a scarab, I always lay a narrow strip of silver paper along one side of the bait to give flash. The scarab has to be wired to keep the bait in position, and for this purpose, as well as wiring the head of the minnow to the lead when the latter has been inserted in the bait, I find 10 amp fuse wire most useful.

TRAPPING MINNOWS.

A supply of minnows for preserving are not always easy to secure unless you live near water which holds a good stock of them. Minnows trap better at some seasons than others. They are usually reluctant I have found on those occasions when you particularly want them. While there are various kinds of minnow traps on the market, the best in my experience is a home-made one. Take a clear glass bottle with an inverted bottom and cut round this with a diamond. Sink the bottle neck downwards in soft earth and tap out the centre of the bottom. This leaves a circular hole which acts as a lead-in for the minnows. Stopper the bottle with a sound, tight-fitting cork. Next tie a length of string to the bottle neck, then bring the remainder back to a little below the centre of the bottle, take a couple of turns and make fast. The rest of the string can then be tied to a wooden float which will mark the position of the bottle when sunk. Place some breadcrumbs in the bottle, fill it with water, and sink it where you can see minnows. In a short time you should have plenty of them. If you then uncork the bottle you can pour them out and sort them according to size. Kill them by putting them into a formalin solution of about a teaspoonful of formalin to a pint of water. The beauty of a trap of this sort is that being clear glass, the minnows can easily see the breadcrumbs.

AMERICAN PLUGS.

American plug baits are now popular on this side of the Atlantic. These baits do not spin, and so cannot twist the line. On the other hand they perform the most weird and wonderful antics in the water, and flash may add to their attractiveness. They are usually painted in various colours, and the latter may also add to their attraction seeing they do not spin. The trouble with them, however, is that the small ones suitable for trout are so light in weight that they cannot be cast fishing distance without the addition of lead on the trace. If some enterprising manufacturer would place a line of small plugs on the market heavy enough without additional lead, I feel sure they would appeal to bait-casting devotees. Personally, after considerable experience of plugs, I much prefer a small spinning bait for trout. Shoud you run out of preserved baits for use with scarab tackle, a few rubber minnows are useful as a standby. To make them, take some thinnish rubber—an old tobacco pouch will do—and mark the outline of a minnow on it. Cut this out with sharp scissors, then repeat the process with another. Next sew the two pieces together with neat stitches, and you have a hollow minnow into which you can insert a lead. Lay a strip of silver paper along one or both sides of the bait, and you will find that it kills quite well when wired in a celluloid scarab.

SPINNING TECHNIQUE.

Upstream spinning with a small quickly-revolving minnow is quite deadly when the water is at summer level. You cast upstream and as the bait reaches its objective you spin it rapidly down so that it is travelling faster than the current. Great accuracy is called for, as you may have to drop your minnow into quite a small area of water. The most likely places to fish are the tails and edges of pools, and the thin streamy water. A run beneath the bank is generally productive of a good trout. In clear water you often see one or more fish following the bait. When this happens, try to keep spinning at an even pace, although the sight of the trout may tempt you to increase the speed. Where there is a run near the bank, cast towards it and spin straight out. If a trout is there he is nearly sure to take. Whether spinning in low water, or when it is clearing after a flood, always keep your minnow coming until it is quite close to you, because a trout may take when the bait is almost at your feet. Much overgrown water can be fished with a deftly thrown minnow that is quite impossible for the fly-fisher. Practice enables you to overcome some very awkward places. As in fly-fishing, never use a longer line than necessary but make as close an approach to your objective as possible. You will be surprised at the size of the trout you get hold of by means of this low-water spinning, good fish which might never leave their hovers to look at a fly, but are tempted to seize the more substantial bait. Most of your time you will be wading, and a short-handled landing net slung on the creel strap will prove useful. Our ancestors used to confine their spinning operations to heavy water, and it would prove a revelation to them could they return and witness the dainty gear used by the modern artist who spins upstream, so different to the coarse tackle employed by the old timers.

Although on occasion the minnow is a very deadly bait, don't imagine it is infallible. The spinner has his good and bad days, just like the fly-fisher, and some of them can be very disappointing indeed, as I know by experience.

HOOKS FOR SPINNING BAITS.

As previously mentioned, the spinning fins on some minnows are too small to enable them to revolve fast enough in slack water, and another fault lies in the fact that their hooks are inadequate. A bait with small hooks may be seized by a trout and let go again, or if the hooks do take a certain amount of hold the fish quickly tears itself free. Some tackle-makers lay stress on the value of small and very sharp hooks when spinning, whereas in reality a size or two larger hook will hold a much greater percentage of fish.

Trout generally take a minnow with great dash, and you can use quite large hooks even on a small bait. A little experience of spinning soon teaches you that trout are cannibals from quite a tender age. Time and again have I taken fish on the minnow that were little larger than the bait itself. Many big cannibal trout, old-stagers that are a real menace to their kind in a small river fall victims to a spinning bait, and are thus well rid of. On the whole you kill a larger percentage of big trout with the minnow than you do with fly, although there are days when the fly makes a handsome contribution to the creel.

A Day's Spinning.

It is very pleasant to find yourself beside the river when the water is clearing after a flood. The rain has gone, leaving blue sky overhead, and a bright sun that makes the raindrops on the grass sparkle like myriad diamonds. Out flies your minnow towards the opposite bank, and after it has gone round and down you reel it back almost to your feet. Again you send it on its journey, still without result, but at about the sixth time of asking you feel a sudden pull and are into a fish. He proves to be a nice half-pounder. You give your trout short shrift on minnow. Time is precious for the water drops back all too quickly. And so you spin downstream for a mile or so, picking up a trout here and another there, until when the inner man craves food you stop to eat your frugal lunch. Before you eat you lift the lid of your creel and slide the contents on to the grass. The count says twenty trout, all nice fish. After lunch you light your pipe and take stock of your surroundings. A dipper flies upstream and settles on a rock, his white waistcoat gleaming in the sunshine. Meadow pipits chirp, and wheatears flit about the old stone walls. From the hillside comes the wailing cry of a curlew, while in the middle distance a kestrel hangs on almost motionless wings, its keen eyes searching the ground beneath for field voles. Over the water a number of red spinners rise and fall, and you note the splash of a trout as it takes an insect near the edge of a pool. Its time to be up and doing again, so you rather reluctantly leave your comfortable seat in the sun and pick up the rod. You wander on downstream taking fair toll of the fish as you go, and by the time you decide to call it a day, there are thirteen more trout in the creel.

If you are spinning the beck with a fly-rod you can work so far downstream and then fish back with fly, but if you start with your spinning outfit it means carrying your fly-rod slung on your shoulder if you wish to change to fly on the return journey. Of course if you have a ghillie to carry the extra rod, well and good, but I'm afraid we can't all run to such luxuries nowadays.

CARING FOR THE LINE AND REEL.

On returning home after a day's spinning run off your line on to a drier. In the case of gut substitute, soak it well before winding it back on your reel. A strip of wet tape wound round the spool will keep the line damp. The tape can be held in position by means of a rubber band. When you get to the river the line will then be soft enough to run through the rod rings without curling. Should you omit to put on the wet tape, attach the line to a piece of wood, make a cast, and let the line soak in the river for a few minutes. It will then be soft enough to reel in, and you can tie on your trace and minnow. Test your line every so often, because the strain and friction on the last few yards is apt to weaken it. Should it break easily, cut off the weak part. Gut substitute makes useful traces. The use of very fine lines and traces when spinning for trout with gut substitute is not to be recommended. Such lines soon wear. A breaking strain of say 4 lbs. is much better. Such a line is not too thick for use in clear water, and gives you ample power over heavy fish. With it you can bring considerable pressure to bear and so save valuable time on a day when the trout are taking minnow really well. Let your swivels be small as long as they do their work properly. Oil them now and then, and see that they work freely. Look after your spinning reel when you get home. Grit and sand have a knack of finding their way into the working parts, especially if you use a fixed spool reel with exposed gears. Keep the latter well oiled so as to reduce wear and tear. Dry your reel thoroughly after a day in the rain, otherwise rust or white oxide will soon make its appearance.

TRACES AND TACKLES.

When making up gut substitute traces, soak the gut until it is thoroughly soft before tying it to the swivels. Diagrams of two knots are appended. Traces showing signs of wear should be scrapped. New ones can be made in a few minutes. Hook tackle should be kept dry, or the hooks will soon rust. When using scarab tackle never leave the hooks attached to the scarab after fishing, because the damp from the minnow is sure to rust them. The more you look after your outfit, the longer will it last.

You need a receptacle of some sort in which to carrx your spinning baits. If they are jumbled up together they get in a horrible mess. Tackle boxes are expensive things to buy, but if you can use a soldering iron it is not difficult to make your own. Cut strips of tin and solder them into a square or oblong baccy tin, thus forming partitions in which each bait can be kept separately. Dry the tin when you get home otherwise it will rust. A coat of enamel will help to protect it, and also make it look a more professional job.

MAKING BAITS AND LEADS.

Home-made minnows kill quite as well as the professional articles. They can be manufactured from lengths of metal tubing, with celluloid or metal fins attached. Give them a plain coat of

How to Fish the Worm.

I like a gut cast tapering to 3x or 4x, about 2½yds. in length. When trout run pretty heavy 3x is best. The reason I prefer a short cast to the usual 9 ft. length is because a good part of the reel line is visible, and when a trout seizes the worm tremors in the line are seen at once, and you know when to strike. You can bait the worm on a single hook or the three-hook Stewart tackle. I prefer the latter because with a single hook you must allow an interval for the trout to get the worm well into its mouth, and this means that the fish often gorges the hook, and time is wasted in extracting it. With the Stewart tackle you can strike at the first touch, and the hooks will be found in the trout's mouth. To bait the single hook, let the worm cover it, leaving the surplus to hang free beyond the point. With the Stewart tackle you can stick the hooks into the worm anywhere. The great art in upstream worming is to allow the worm to trundle down the bed of the river at the will of the current. No shot is required on the cast, as the worm is heavy enough itself. You cast the worm by a forward underhand swing, or a side swing. When the water is at summer level, trout lie in the shallow streams and runs between stones. Although the worm is deadly in low water, there are days when trout come short at it. Why this should be so I cannot say. I have made some of my heaviest baskets in the early morning, but trout often take worm well during the heat of the day. Having cast to a likely spot, or to a fish visible in the shallows, you let the current bring the worm down while you raise the point of the rod, so as to keep the line fairly tight. When a trout takes, the worm stops, and you see a tremor of the line. Now and then the worm is held up by a stone or other obstacles, but experience enables you to decide between such a contretemps and a taking fish.

Upstream worming can be hard work during the hottest part of the day, because you have to bend your back and keep as low as possible when approaching your objective, but it is well worth a few aches and pains to feel your creel becoming heavier and heavier on your shoulder. The angler whose holiday is limited to the yearly fortnight will do well to cultivate the art of upstream worming for it may be that when he arrives at his destination, he finds the water has shrunk to its lowest level, and fly-fishing during the day is a somewhat thankless job. Under these conditions he can fish the worm from daybreak onwards, and then change to fly at the approach of dusk.

Worms for Bait.

Worms for clear-water work should be scoured and toughened, otherwise they don't last long. First wash your worms, then place them in a jar filled with moss. The latter ahould also be washed and wrung out. At intervals the jar should be examined, and if you find any dead or

weakly looking worms, throw them away.
Change the moss, too, from time to time.
Worms are generally carried in a moss filled bag
which you can attach to a button of your jacket.
There is also on the market a tin box which you
can attach to a waist belt. It has two com-
partments, the larger of which holds the worms,
while the other contains fine sand into which
you can dip your fingers before handling the baits.

There is no more pleasant time to be beside
the stream than on a June morning at daybreak.
The mist still hangs above the hill-tops, giving
promise of a hot day to come, and the dew lies
heavy on the grass, so that you can see the plainly
marked trails left by the rabbits during their
night's wanderings. Before the sun gains power
the air is clear and cool, enabling you to distinguish the many countryside scents, some of
which, like that of the hawthorn, are particularly
strong. Even at that early hour insect life is
prolific, and dew-spangled spiders' webs festoon
the hedges.

Perhaps a lordly cock pheasant strides into view,
the early morning sun glinting on his gaudy
plumage. Rooks pass back and forth, the young
ones hatched in May now flying strongly. Most
wild life is abroad at that hour, but as the sun gets
higher, the four-footed creatures seek out their
day-time retreats. By the time your inner man
calls for food, you will be glad to wade ashore
and find a shady place in which to eat your lunch.
Having fed, you light your pipe, and rest awhile.

PLATE VI

A good pool on a Yorkshire Beck.

As our American cousins say: "It is not all of fishing just to fish!" for during the interludes of sport, many and varied are the sights and sounds of the countryside, all of which add greatly to the pleasure of an angler's day.

THE STONEFLY A KILLING BAIT.

Another very killing bait for trout is the stonefly and its larva, the "creeper." Scientifically known as Perla Bicaudata, the stonefly is an ugly brute, but quite harmless. It spends its larval state beneath the water. Trout take both the fully matured fly and the "creeper" with avidity. The male stonefly is known as the "jack." It is unable to rise from the ground, and the female is no great shakes when it comes to using her wings. In late May and early June you can find hundreds of stoneflies which have hatched out on the gravel beds of our north-country becks. You have only to turn up the stones at the water's edge in order to collect all you require in the way of bait. Trout are on the watch for stoneflies after a slight rise of water has washed them out of their retreats. Should a flood arrive, the stonefly crop is carried away altogether.

FISHING THE STONEFLY.

You fish the natural "creeper" or stonefly, like you do the upstream worm. You can use the same rod, line, and cast, with a special two-hook tackle to hold the bait. The tackle consists

E

of two hooks, about 5/8th inch apart, and on opposite sides of the gut. The upper hook is a No. 2, and the lower a No. 3. To bait, pass the upper hook through the throat of the fly, and push the lower one through its abdomen. To fish the stonefly, choose if possible a day with an upstream wind, and an inch or two of fresh water in the beck. Streams and broken water are likely places, as are the fringes of the gravel beds. Should there be a good breeze you may take some trout from the pools. Having collected sufficient flies, keep them in a box from which you can easily extract one at a time. There is a useful zinc box on the market which can be carried on a waist belt.

There are various patterns of artificial stonefly to be had, but none of them can, as far as my experience goes, compete with the natural insect.

THE BRACKEN CLOCK BEETLE.

Another good trout bait is the bracken clock beetle. Thousands of these beetles appear amongst the fern in June, and any which fall on the water are greedily taken by the fish. Amongst the standard flies the Coch-y-bondhu is supposed to represent this beetle. While I have killed trout with the Coch-y-bondhu, I much prefer a floating model known as " Kennedy's Beetle." This is an excellent imitation of the bracken clock, in fact one of the few artificial baits that kill really well. I don't say it is the equal of the natural beetle, all the same, I have killed some good baskets of trout with it during bracken clock time.

The beetle that we in the north call the bracken clock is known in parts of Wales as the Coch-y-bondhu. There seems, however, to be some confusion regarding the latter's natural prototype. Other local names besides bracken clock are, fern webb, shorn fly, marlow buzz, etc. The name Coch-y-bondhu is Welsh, and means, I believe, red-black-red. As a matter of fact the red cowdung beetle tallies better with the de-description red-black-red than the bracken clock. In scientific language the latter is called Phyllopertha horticola. Various other beetles such as the soldier beetle, sailor beetle, cowdung beetle, etc., are attractive to trout. Artificials of these beetles can be tied after the manner of the standard trout flies, or imitated in what I may term the natural-artificial manner. Certain beetles tied in the latter fashion are quite killing. Using natural bracken clocks, as well as "Kennedy's Beetle," I have had good baskets of trout from various mountain tarns and reservoirs. Tied as a fly, the Coch-y-bondhu is well known. You can dress it as follows: body, peacock and black ostrich herl twisted and run down together and ribbed with gold. Hackle, dark furnace cock's from tail to head.

On any rough river where there happens to be a hatch of Mayflies or Green Drakes, the natural fly will kill trout, which reminds me that when anglers from north and south foregather, there may be some confusion over the term Mayfly. The northerner generally applies that name to the stonefly, whereas the south country angler refers to the handsome green drake. Nowadays wherever there is a hatch of Mayflies the black-headed gulls seem to find them. I have noticed these gulls on Lake Windermere take nearly every Mayfly that appeared.

The maggot is a bait that trout are fond of. Dead sheep and other carcasses lying in the water get fly-blown, and the maggots that are carried down by the current are soon picked up by the fish. I remember a visiting angler who made a great killing on a Lakeland beck some years ago with maggots. He used quite a lot of them for ground bait, and made a clean-up of some big trout which inhabited a certain pool, besides numbers of smaller fish.

Flies like the blue-bottle, and the wood fly, can be used when dapping for trout, while various caterpillars prove acceptable. The chief baits used on our northern becks, however, are the worm, stonefly, and bracken clock beetle. With them, plus artificial fly and minnow, the angler is kept busy throughout the season.

While natural baits may not appeal to the dyed-in-the-wool fly-fisherman, the more liberal minded angler is not so pernickety. There are days when in the north of England for example bracken clock beetles absolutely swarm in the fern besides the becks, and a goodly supply can be gathered in a few minutes. Nobody but a fool

salmon. I began to spin after the tide turned, but beyond touching two fish, and having a strong pull from a third which came unstuck, I did nothing. My brother-in-law and my wife were with me, and they had several touches, as did two other anglers, but not a fish was landed. The day was hot with a fair breeze, and everything seemed ideal for sport. Just to show how the luck falls, on October 18th of the same year, my wife killed eight sea trout and lost three others, while I had several touches and did nothing. She killed all her fish in a channel about fifty yards long. It was a sunny day, with a north-east breeze on and off. The river was in nice order after rain, with no tide.

When spinning for sea trout there is always the chance of getting into a salmon. Slobs, as previously mentioned, may also be taken. A really silvery slob can easily be mistaken for a sea trout, and a big sea trout for a small salmon, or a small salmon for a big sea trout unless you know the characters to look for. On October 18th, 1934, my brother-in-law killed a 10 lb. 1 oz. fish in the Leven which at first glance appeared to be a salmon, but a closer inspection revealed it as a female sea trout, $6\frac{1}{2}$ years old, with three spawning marks. It was taken in tidal water on a natural minnow. A 4 lb. fish from the same river was deemed to be a sea trout, but scale examination proved it was a grilse. Mention has already been made of the 2 lb. $10\frac{1}{2}$ oz slob trout which was at first taken for a fresh-run sea trout.

DISTINGUISHING MARKS.

There are various tests to distinguish between sea trout and salmon, the best you can use at the river being the scale count, and the shape of the anal fin, which is more pointed in the sea trout than the salmon. The number of scales in an oblique line drawn downwards and forward from the hind edge of the adipose fin to the lateral line is 10 to 13 (usually 11) in the salmon, and 13 to 16 (usually 14, rarely 12) in the trout.

Sea trout, like brown trout, have their favourite lying places. On the tidal reaches these lying places may change, because the banks are sandy, and sand is a moveable quantity. Floods and tides work their will on it, with the result that the course of the river alters. When the stream is in flood and the tides are low, the water forms channels and washes them out until their stony and gravelly beds are exposed. It is in these channels where there is usually a good current and the water is fairly shallow, that the sea trout and salmon prefer to lie.

Then the high tides come, bringing twenty or more feet of water, and when next you go down to fish your favourite channel you find it has been silted up, and the river is running under the opposite bank. Under favourable conditions, however, a well cleaned out channel may remain in situ throughout the greater part of the season, especially where the bank has been reinforced by stones to prevent erosion.

When fishing the tidal reaches it is wise to

watch your step, because where the sand has been flooded by high tide it takes a long time to dry and harden, thus quicksands are formed which suck you down unexpectedly. Even if you only go in to your knees, it is a horrible sensation, and you may have considerable difficulty in freeing yourself.

FLASHING FLY AND BAIT.

Bright coloured flies are the best for sea trout, flies that give plenty of flash. The same applies to a minnow. When using a natural minnow in scarab tackle I lay a strip of silver paper along one side of the bait in order to increase flash. Although sea trout in tidal water may take a certain number of natural insects, their chief food consists of sprats, sand-eels, etc., and a minnow kills because it doubtless affords a sufficiently good representation of such food. When really in the mood for taking, sea trout use no more discrimination than brown trout. They will seize a minnow, or some gaudy contraption of feather and tinsel without the slightest hesitation. Red-letter days with sea trout are, in my experience, quite as few and far apart as they are with brown trout, in fact further apart. In tidal water at any rate, if you get half-a-dozen really good days during the season, you are lucky.

SPINNING TECHNIQUE.

I prefer minnow in the tidal reaches because you can cover far more water than when using fly. In my experience, the natural minnow in scarab tackle kills better than an artificial bait. While an ordinary Devon, or one of reflex pattern, will account for both sea trout and salmon, the natural seems to have just that little bit extra about it that makes it more effective. Perhaps it is the smell that scores. Both my wife and I use fixed spool reels and gut substitute lines of 6 lbs. breaking strain. On the open water of the tidal reaches where there are no rocks or other obstructions, you can bring your fish to net in well under a minute to the pound. Using a 6 lbs. line you can set the clutch so as to afford considerable tension that soon makes even the liveliest fish see reason. To adjust the tension pull off a yard or so of line over the flier eye. If you then feel a fair amount of resistance the tension will be about right. A little experience soon teaches you how to set the clutch control on the face of the line drum properly. In order to take full advantage of the reel's casting power, always keep the spool so filled with line that the latter comes just under the inside edge of the drum. This avoids friction on the lip of the spool. Should the line be too short, friction will greatly reduce your casting distance.

In my experience the sea trout is our gamest and most sporting fish. Hook him and he runs hard, generally ending his dash by a spectacular jump. Up and out he shoots like a bar of silver as the sun glints on his scales, then back he goes with a resounding splash, amidst a shower of glittering drops. When he finally comes to hand and you lay him on the grass, what a picture he makes. Surely the old Highlanders were right when they said he was one of the three things lovely in death.

ON THE TIDAL WATERS.

When you leave the hill-streams and rocky becks for the tidal reaches, near the estuary, you find yourself in a very different environment. You are in a land of low-lying fields through which the river meanders between sandy banks on its way to the sea. For the most part the current runs slower than it does on the upper reaches, but there is still plenty of fast water in the channels where the mignatory fish love to lie.

Fauna and flora are different, too. The hill-birds are absent, and in their place you see wild-fowl and shore birds. Mallard and teal visit the sandy reaches, and boldly marked shelducks often put in an appearance. You hear the whistle of oyster catchers, the alarm notes of redshanks, and the hoarse laughter of the blackbacked gulls as they squabble over some tit-bit cast up by the tide. Sometimes a kingfisher flashes past on its way upstream, a veritable feathered jewel. Herons stand like sentinels on the sandy promontories, so still that they can almost be mistaken for posts. Flocks of green plover wheel and settle in the fields, where sometimes you may see a lordly cock pheasant from the nearby woods.

Partridges are there, too, and towards evening, you may hear them calling. Carrion crows, rooks and jackdaws also visit the river, for they know that many a tasty morsel can be picked up after the tide has receded and left the sandbanks bare. Otters regularly haunt the tidal reaches, and you see their five-toed imprints in the sand. The tracks of rats are numerous, too, as well as those of rabbits.

Reeds and rushes whisper in the wind, and where the fields edge the river banks, sea-pinks bloom profusely. On the upper tidal reaches, woods stretch down to the water. Blackberries are plentiful, often growing to a large size, and a basket of mushrooms is often procurable from the fields. The air is fresh and strong with the tang of the sea, making the tidal country a happy hunting ground for the angler. As our American cousins say: " It is not all of fishing just to fish!" And nowhere does this better apply than on the tidal reaches where nature provides so much of interest.

As already mentioned, migratory fish run with the tide, and on a sunny day when a north-west wind kicks the water into wavelets, you may see both salmon and trout show themselves freely on their journey upstream. Time after time a living bar of silver shoots into the air, to fall back again in a graceful curve, or land with a smack that sends the water flying. It makes your mouth water to watch them, and you hope you may have the luck to get into a fish or two after the tide has turned.

As a rule, however, one has the best sport on a day when there is no tide, but the river is running a nice height after rain. When a flood arrives the water becomes thick, with sand, and it takes a day or more to clear sufficiently for spinning. Given a sunny day, a good breeze and a nice water, you have every right to expect some decent sport. Incidentally, you can hardly have too much wind when spinning, especially should the water be on the low side.

SPINNING A CHANNEL.

Having arrived at your favourite channel you put the rod together and attach a minnow in its neat celluloid scarab. There is a nice water and you commence operations at the head of the channel where the river narrows, forming a fast run. Out goes the bait to fall with a tiny splash under the far bank. The pull of the current swings it round and down and you reel it in almost to your feet. Moving on a couple of yards you cast again. Still nothing happens. At the fifth time of asking you feel a pull, but the fish—a whitling, known in the north as a sprod—comes unstuck. Far down the channel a sea trout jumps, evidence that fish are in, and at that moment as if to confirm the fact, you get a real good tug. This time the hooks go home, and the fish makes a quick run ending with a spectacular leap. You pump him back, and he runs again. The reel tension is too much for him, however, and in a very short time he comes in and you draw him

over the net.   He proves to be a sea trout of just
over 2 lbs., a perfect bar of silver.   You slip
him into the bag, and carry on.   Twice you feel a
touch, probably small fish, then a sprod takes
hold.   You pull him straight in, a little fellow of
13 oz.   Two or three minutes later you hook
another sprod, but he jumps and comes unstuck.
Cast follows cast until about half-way down the
channel you get a heavy pull.   The fish runs
hard towards the further bank, and when he stops
you pump him back.   Again he runs, and again,
but the pressure tells, until finally you have him
close in.   A final flurry, then you bring him
head-first into the net and draw him ashore
where you tap him on the napper with the priest.
This time your quarry is a salmon, a nice little
fish of 7 lbs. 6 oz.   Five minutes later another
sea trout takes hold.   He goes through the usual
acrobatics, then just as you bring him in the hold
gives, and he quietly disappears.   Hard luck, as
he looked to be at least a two-pounder.   You
change the minnow for one with a reverse spin,
light a pipe, and try again.   Shortly another sprod
comes to hand, then near the end of the channel
where the river shallows over stones before
entering a deep pool, a good fish takes.   He
emulates the salmon's tactics, but doesn't last as
long, and finally you net a sea trout of 3½ lbs., a
bonny fish.   In the pool below a salmon jumps
but is beyond your reach, for at this point a tri-
butary stream enters the river, and you cannot
cross it owing to quicksands and deep water,

PLATE VII

A pool below a natural dam on a Lakeland beck.

so you turn back to your starting point. Fishing accounts can be tedious, so suffice it to say that by the time you feel like lunch, three more fish have been accounted for, two sprods and a sea trout of $1\frac{1}{2}$ lbs.

You find a comfortable seat with your back against the grassy bank and get out the sandwiches and a bottle of beer. Having fed, you light your pipe, and take it easy for half-an-hour. Across the river several oyster-catchers are moving about. Downstream a cormorant suddenly appears in the pool where the salmon jumped. It finally comes ashore and spreads its wings to dry. Two shelducks pass overhead shortly followed by several wood pigeons. The latter swerve sharply as they spot you under the bank. Somewhere the black-backed gulls are wrangling, probably over the carcass of a sheep left high and dry by the tide. It is very pleasant in the sun, and the sea air makes you feel drowsy, but you have come to fish, so you pick up your gear and make your way upstream to where a bridge spans the river. Above the bridge there is a good channel, and you start at the head of it. The first reach is shallow, and in it you hook and land another sprod. Lower down the river deepens until it meets more shallows under the bridge. As you near the latter you have a clear view of a salmon as he rises at the minnow, but for some reason or other doesn't take. You try him again but there is nothing doing, and you have to be content with a sprod that comes to net under the bridge.

F

As things are you decide it is better to go back to your old channel, so return downstream and try it again.   The result is two fish, a sea trout of $1\frac{1}{2}$ lbs. and another sprod, which makes your bag for the day just a dozen fish.   You are more than satisfied as you make your way to the main road where you pick up a bus for home.

CHAPTER VII

THE WEATHER

THE fly-fisherman generally has some excuse for an empty creel. He will tell you that the air was too cold and no insects appeared; the sun was too bright, thunder was about, or the wind blew downstream when it should have been blowing up, in fact anything to account for the void beneath his basket lid. The idea is prevalent amongst anglers that insects only hatch when weather conditions are propitious. Let us glance for a moment at the theory that a hatch only materializes when the weather permits, and that severe cold is inimical to filling a creel.

Most north-country fishermen who begin the season in March know how sometimes the March Browns rise in swarms when weather conditions are extremely severe, so severe in fact that unless you have witnessed such a rise you can hardly believe that delicate insects could survive and finally take wing. Under such conditions when your feet and hands are numb, fishing is not perhaps a pleasant prospect, yet if you brave the elements you can kill plenty of trout on fly.

ANGLING AND COLD WEATHER.

With regard to the appearance of insects, the latter come from eggs, and the eggs hatch in their due time irrespective of the weather. If March Browns appear during an Arctic spell, there is great reason to suppose that the eggs of other insects hatch in like manner under similar conditions. In " Fishermen's Weather," the late Sir Herbert Maxwell says that the regular rise of trout " is dependent on the rise of fly, and that, of some species, seems to depend on season and hour of day irrespective of weather. For instance, one March, on a bitter blustery day, with driving snow and the river full of floating and fixed ice, there was a tremendous rise of March Browns on the Helmsdale, which the trout were ravenously devouring, though the water temperature was only 35°F. No angler would have found any encouragement in the text-books to go forth under such a sky. Yet he might have filled a basket. The biggest rise of March Browns I ever saw was on the Tay in April, 1905; weather, bitter, with hard north wind. The river was alive with rising trout."

BRIGHT SUN NO DETRIMENT.

When it comes to the light, many a fly-fisherman will tell you that too much sun is bad for sport. " Give me a dull day," he will say. And yet, if you turn the pages of a well-kept diary, you will find there are many records of sunny, cloudless days on which sport was first-rate. Let me quote one or two instances from my own diary. An April day, clear, and hot sun, with a light southerly breeze. Trout took well, killed

50. A day in July. Bright sun and warm. Wind north-west. Glass high and steady. Nice fly-water. Total 57 trout. A June day, clear and hot. Light north-west breeze, later became strong and gusty. Nice fly-water after rain two days before. Trout took very well. Killed 125. Sometimes you hear that the weather is too hot. Again the diary refutes it. I find that on a blazing hot day in July with no breeze and clouds of natural fly, the trout rose well and 61 were creeled.

WIND AND THUNDER.

Wind may, of course, be a help or drawback on the river. If you are fishing upstream against a stiff breeze, you may have trouble in presenting your flies. On the other hand such a wind is an aid to fishing the still pools, because it ruffles the surface and trout take a chance which they otherwise would not do if the water was calm. Wind also helps to refresh the water and this refreshment has an influence on trout. The excuse that thunder was about has considerable truth in it, because before a thunderstorm the atmosphere is enervating. We ourselves feel dull and languid then, while cattle and sheep often cease feeding. I have often wondered whether at such times the conditions of the atmosphere makes the grass distasteful to them? Most wild things are more or less dull before a storm. Trout suffer from the depression, and under the influence of thunder become almost impossible to move.

There are certain exceptions in fish life, however. Eels come forth from their lairs before a thunderstorm, and char are on the feed.

HIGH AND LOW PRESSURE.

Both thermometer and barometer are affected by a change. Is the trout's mood influenced by temperature? It seems doubtful. Trout often rise well when the thermometer is low, as witness the appearance of March Browns, previously mentioned. They do the same, too, when it is high and the weather hot. The same applies to medium temperatures. Only in one way does temperature seem to affect the fish, and that is in their choice of lying places. Before a storm it is the low pressure that tends to make the air decay and gives us " that tired feeling." Let the storm break, however, with a torrential downpour, and what a change ensues. The trout which had previously ignored your flies begin to come at them like wolves, and they continue to do so as long as the mercury in the barometer rises. Why, you may ask, do the fish show such a sudden change of mind. The answer is, I think, because a storm clears the air and revivifies the trout, just as it does animals and human beings. When the storm breaks the pressure is low, and the glass soon begins to rise. When it becomes high and stationary the trout may take less eagerly, or not at all. This seems to point to the fact that it is not high pressure that makes them keen and provides us with our few red-letter days. No, the condition that makes trout ravenous for our flies seems to be the sudden increase of pressure. As previously mentioned in the case of the March Browns, sport is sometimes good during a snowy period. At such a time the temperature is low or falling, but the glass is rising. Under pressure a fluid will absorb gas. Reduce the pressure and some of the air escapes. The deep water in a river is less affected than the shallows because it is under the greater pressure of the water above it, and being colder than the surface water it absorbs some of the air from it. For this reason a trout near the surface fails to find sufficient aeration, and so retires to the deep water until conditions change. The fish is on a par with the mountaineer who finds that the higher he climbs, the less the air pressure. For this reason he may have difficulty in breathing, and if he forces himself to go on he will collapse because his heart cannot stand the strain.

Trout are without doubt extraordinarily susceptible to atmospheric influences. Nothing but the influence of atmospherical conditions could make trout rise en masse and then cease feeding at a given signal. It is not hunger that brings them to your flies on one of the few red-letter days, because every fish you hook is crammed with food, yet they go on rising madly.

When all is said and done, our enjoyment of the sport of fishing is dependent upon the differing conditions of the atmosphere. If, as mentioned in a previous chapter, we knew we were going to fill a creel to overflowing every time we went out, we should very soon tire of fly-fishing, and turn to something else that would provide us with a greater measure of uncertainty.   The dyed-in-the-wool trout fisherman is something like the keen foxhunter who when asked what were the three things he liked best on earth, replied, " a good day with foxhounds, a bad day with foxhounds, and then—damn it all, sir, a *blank* day with foxhounds."

In the previous chapter on " Trout flies," I have given examples from my own diary of those all too infrequent red-letter days that we so eagerly look forward to.   These days only come when atmospherical conditions are propitious, or in other words, the state of the pressure is favourable.   Anglers may blame the sun, wind, cold, heat or snow for their non-success, but such are not the actual causes of failure.

A THUNDER STORM.

How often, after a period of almost unbearably sultry weather, have I watched the dark clouds gathering amongst the hills.   Over everything hung a great silence, as if the world was waiting with bated breath.   Suddenly the heavens were split by a flash of lightning, followed by the reverberating roar of thunder.   Then great raindrops like " pennies from heaven " began to fall, and soon a deluge was descending.   Parched runners came to life, and the fellsides were marked by silver streaks where the flood water was rushing down to join the parent stream. Swiftly the water in the latter rose until it was running a brown flood. Then the rain ceased, the last mutter of thunder died away, and the sun shone. Raindrops glittered like diamonds on the grass, and steam rose from the drenched earth. Big trout had left their hiding places and were foraging for worms. In an hour or two the water began to clear, and I made my way to the beck, confident that the refreshment of the atmosphere would bring the trout eagerly to my flies. Even in the north amongst the hills storms are infrequent, and so are the red-letter days, because it needs an outbreak of the elements to provide us with those atmospheric conditions that enliven the trout and rouse them into taking. Perhaps for days, or even weeks, before the storm, a basket of trout was practically impossible with fly, although it could perhaps be done by carefully fishing a well scoured worm upstream. What a relief it was when the rain came, and the feeling of oppression disappeared. It is easy to understand therefore, how the wet-fly fisherman cherishes these all too few red-letter occasions, and makes the most of them. Forgotten are the blank or near blank days when a brace or two were your meagre reward for patient casting. Now you get a rise at almost every throw, and occasionally net a couple of trout at once which have seized both tail fly and dropper.

As the water clears you may see numbers of red spinners dancing in the sunlight, with here and there flies of many other species. The spinners may be well in the majority, but that is no reason why you need fish with an artificial that supposedly represents them. By far the greater number of trout are taking nymphs of various kinds, and that is why your wet flies kill so well. Lightly tied, they afford an impressionistic idea of underwater fare such as the fish delight in, and the trout of the fast water do not pick and choose. It is a case of " that's food—that was," unless a fish times his rush to a split second. No, use any pattern of artificial that you have confidence in, and you will fill a basket as long as the advantageous conditions provided by the storm remain in being.

CHAPTER VIII

CONFIDENCE

FISHING a hill stream one day, I met a visiting angler. He was a stranger to me, and after enquiring about sport, he asked me what flies I was using. I replied two Black Spinners. Then followed the expected question, why use two flies of similar pattern? My answer was, because I had confidence in them! I explained to him how for many years the Black Spinner had helped me to kill quite as many trout per season as in former years a score or more of patterns had, and that the use of one or two flies in which you have confidence saves no end of time that would otherwise be spent in changing, while it keeps the flies in the water where they should be. I also hinted that trout in fast water have little time to pick and choose, nor are they particular as regards the edible matter brought down by the current. I don't think he was convinced, so after a pleasant chat we parted and went our separate ways.

I lay stress on the matter of confidence, for when you come to think of it, it plays a most important part in angling. As a matter of fact it is more than half the battle. The art of presentation, too, helps tremendously. It is the man with " hands " who presents his flies in the most seductive manner. If he has perfect confidence in his flies, then he will be at the top of his form when it comes to presenting them. On many occasions since I first started using two flies, I have been asked by various visiting anglers to try certain patterns of theirs. In most instances I have endeavoured to give these flies as fair a trial as possible, but when using them I have seldom felt at ease, for the simple reason that something was lacking, that something being confidence. All the time I was hankering to put my own favourite back on the cast. Without real confidence in your flies you will never fish them as they should be fished. I always think that the man who is for ever changing his flies can have little confidence in any of them, and his season's total of fish must suffer considerably in consequence.

When spinning I have the same feeling. Unless I am using a natural minnow, my confidence in the lure wanes. I have killed salmon with a silver reflex bait, and plenty of brown trout with a quill minnow, but I have more confidence in the natural than any of the artificials. It is the same when fishing in salt water for pollack. Then my two favourite lures are a white fly, and a rubber sand-eel.

It is success with any particular fly or bait that inspires confidence. There are days, of course, when your chosen patterns are practically ignored, yet you go on fishing with the feeling that it isn't the fault of the flies, but that some subtle change in the atmosphere is responsible.

STRENGTH OF MIND.

As mentioned in a previous chapter, it takes some strength of mind to break away from the change-fly habit, yet once you do so you will find that you quickly acquire confidence in the flies you choose for the experiment. It's a queer thing this feeling of confidence. Something you can't exactly describe. If you have it, you fish your flies serenely without any lingering doubt that something else might do better. It helps enormously towards filling a creel, and saves valuable time, not to mention money, because very few flies are needed to see you through a season. Of course if you tie your own flies, expense is still further reduced.

While confidence and presentation are more than half the battle, even the most expert fly-fisherman cannot fill a creel unless conditions are favourable. Why, you may ask, does an angler plug away day after day with little or no result? The answer is that he hopes sport will improve. He never knows when it may do so, and this uncertainty keeps him going. In it lies the great charm of angling. If it were cut and dried so that you know beforehand you were going to fill your creel every time you went out, the uncertainty would be gone, and with it the interest. It is the same with other field sports. If you knew that hounds would kill every fox they found, or that every horse you back would be automatically returned a winner, the thrill would evaporate. Unless you get a kick out of things they are apt to fall flat. Nature is strange and mysterious in her ways. It seems reasonable to suppose that she has so arranged matters that the angler will retain interest in his sport. Were it otherwise, not only would the fisherman soon tire, but he and his kind would do such execution amongst the trout that their ranks would soon be unduly thinned if not decimated. Thus the arrangement that helps to retain the angler's interest, works also for the benefit of the trout, inasmuch as it protects them from their own greed.

CHAPTER IX

IMPROVING THE BECK

ON the average beck whose birth-place is far up amongst the hills, the trout are plentiful but small. A stream of this kind is subject to sudden floods, and for that reason little in the way of trout food can find a resting place, with the exception of caddis and the water moss which clings to the rocks. Trout cannot be expected to thrive and grow unless they are adequately fed, and as the beck is short of food until such time as various larvæ and insects materialize in summer, it is up to you to do something about it if you wish to improve both the trout and the fishing.

Take a walk up the beck from the point where it enters the parent river to its source near the fell head, and you will find, particularly on the upper reaches, terraced formations where the water cascades out of one pool into another. When you fish the beck, each of these pools will generally provide you with a trout, and sometimes two or three. In between these rocky lengths are long, gravelly shallows where you seldom make contact with a trout. Why, you may ask, do the fish inhabit the pools and not the shallows? The answer is because the pools form larders in which food accumulates, whereas on the shallows that feel the full force of the floods, food is scarce, and there are no resting places for the fish if they wished to remain there.   Trout, like ourselves, need rest, they can't keep on bucking the current all the time, and it is for this reason you find them in those terraced pools where food, rest and shelter are provided free of charge.

While re-stocking works well enough in rivers which can supply the new-comers with food, it is a hopeless undertaking on the beck where the trout are already too plentiful for the existing commisariat.   No, the only way in which you can improve both your trout and your fishing is to provide more pools, and in consequence, more food.

The existing terraced pools are formed by natural stone dams.   If you want more pools of a similar nature, you must be prepared to undertake some pretty strenuous work with pick and crowbar; while the labour is hard, as I know from experience in my younger days when I did a good deal of it on a Yorkshire beck, it is most interesting and well worth while.   If the stream is small you can do quite a lot single-handed, but on the average beck you need one or more helpers.

While dams can be constructed of concrete, boards, logs, wattle, or plain wire-netting against which rubbish gradually accumulates, such work needs money, and in the case of concrete, professional labour.   On the beck your materials are already to hand in the shape of rocks and boulders which you can shift into position by the sweat of your brow and your own unpaid labour.

PLATE VIII

Fishing a moorland beck in Yorkshire.

The first thing is to select sites for your dams. Here and there you may find a rough line of deeply embedded rocks and boulders already across the stream. That is the place to start building, for the main foundations are already in situ, and all you have to do is fill in the gaps with other rocks and smaller stuff.

" All you have to do!" says you. Well it certainly means that you must take your coat off and roll up your sleeves, and I grant you the work is not exactly easy. Once you acquire the knack of wielding pick and bar, however, you will be surprised how much you can get done in a day. Let your pick be a really strong and hefty one, because you will do most of the work with it.

Both above and below the site of your proposed dam, you will find rocks and boulders, but you need only pay attention to those above, because it is much easier to move them downstream with the current than up against it from below. The first thing you will discover when you begin to shift rocks, is that they are embedded far more deeply in the river-bed than you expected. Here is where the pick gets in its good work. Drive it in on the upstream side of the boulder you wish to move until it gets a grip, then pull back on the handle in the upstream direction. If the leverage is sufficient, the rock should begin to give, and your companion can then hold it with the bar until you get a fresh purchase. Some rocks are so shaped that you can roll them downstream to

G

near the site of your dam without much trouble, while others are ugly customers which take some handling. In the days when I did a good deal of this work, we used to loosen up as many big boulders as we thought we should need for blocking up the main spaces between the boulders already in situ, and then work them down near the dam before we actually began to build it. Once you begin to build and the main foundation rocks are jammed into position, the water naturally rises, but a lot of it still gets through. To stop this, you wedge smaller rocks and stones into the interstices, and jam up any cracks with moss. You will be able to tear plenty of this off rocks in the neighbourhood. All the work is of course, done on the upstream side of the dam. Lastly pile a good supply of smaller boulders along the dam's base, then, if your work has been done properly, you will find yourself standing in a pool, the overflow of which spills over your dam, and forms the head of your next pool should you build another dam further downstream. On the average shallow there is room for a number of rough boulder dams, so that you get pools in terrace formation like those which nature has provided on other reaches.

When building a dam, always remember that it has to withstand the winter floods, thus it behoves you to put as great a weight of stone into it as you can manage, and at the same time see that the key stones are so placed that the force of the flood will only jam them tighter between the boulders that were already in position. The more pains you take over the building of your dams, the longer will they last.

Even a temporary dam will serve to show you how quickly trout appreciate a new-made pool. In my youthful days, before dipping became the vogue, there was a sheepfold on a little Yorkshire beck, adjoining which the shepherds used to dam the water and form a pool in which they washed the members of their flock. Many a time when fishing up the beck I visited that pool, and seldom failed to take a trout or two out of it. The dam was only a semi-permanent affair, most of it being washed away by the first flood.

If, when your permanent boulder dam is built, you are doubtful as to the strength at certain points on the downstream side, you can greatly stiffen the suspected weak spots by driving stout larch posts into the stream bed where they will take the strain when floods materialize.

Having completed your prescribed series of dams, the pools so formed cover a considerable area of gravel that was previously dry when the water was at summer level. This means that a larger breeding ground for aquatic insects has been provided, and that eventually far more food in the shape of shrimps, stoneflies, etc., will be available for the trout. The more gravel you can flood and keep flooded, the bigger crop of aquatic insects you will have. Without your dams much gravel would only be under water when the beck rose, and if stoneflies laid their eggs at such a time, they would soon be left high and dry when the freshet receded. Exactly the same applies to any larvæ which find their way to temporarily flooded areas of gravel.

By forming pools, as above described, you provide breeding grounds for aquatic insects, in which they can find security from floods, and these pools act as larders for the trout which quickly show their appreciation of the new storehouses. In addition to the trout food gained by flooding what would otherwise be unproductive gravel, there are various water plants which add their quota to the general supply. Such plants cannot grow in the beck itself, because they would be promptly swept away by floods.

On the average hill-stream there are patches of wet and swampy ground adjacent to the water, and it is in those situations that you find beds of watercress, marsh-marigolds, etc. On a Westmorland beck which I often fish, water plants of this kind are fairly plentiful, and the food which they supply finds its way to the stream *via* oozy trickles through the sodden ground.

By making new beds of cress, and transplanting marigolds, etc., to suitable situations, you can add considerably to the existing crop of trout food. Wherever watercress grows, there you will find shrimps, and these are a welcome addition to the menu. Here and there on ground adjacent to the beck you find shallow pools in which numbers of frogs breed. As you draw near to one of them you hear a droning sound that is exactly like the distant hum of a motor cycle. Crossing the fell one day with a friend I could hear the music of some frogs, and my companion exclaimed: "How plainly you can hear that motor bike!" I told him it wasn't a motor cycle, but frogs, and at first he wouldn't believe me. However, when we trod softly towards a little pond amongst the peat, he realized it was frogs and saw them disturbing the water. Frogs are susceptible to vibrations, and they immediately cease their concert when they realize your presence. Later you will find the pools full of glutinous masses amongst which are black dots. These dots are frogs' eggs enclosed in large swollen globes of jelly. They first hatch into tadpoles with hind-legs, then the front legs appear, after which they become tiny frogs and take to land. Trout are fond of both tadpoles and young frogs when they can get them. If you find a tadpole nursery some yards distant from the beck, you can provide the trout with a bonne bouche by cutting a trench from the pool to the river. As the pool gradually empties, the tadpoles are carried down the trench, and when they reach the beck, the trout soon realize that manna from heaven has mysteriously appeared. Nature is of necessity wasteful. She has to be in order that sufficient numbers of eggs should survive. I have often found masses of frog spawn in high-lying pools on the hills, but on passing that way later some of the pools had dried up and the spawn was destroyed.

In some reaches of the beck you see small blue and red dragonflies, with now and then one of the larger species that is four inches or so across the wings. Trout sometimes take the smaller flies. The larvæ of the large dragonfly are most carniverous, and do considerable damage to other sub-aquatic creatures. In summer the chirping of grasshoppers is a common sound beside the beck. It is not chirping really, but stridulation, because the sound is made by rubbing the shoulder-blades together. Grasshoppers are good bait for trout. In June, as you fish upstream towards the headwaters, you will see hundreds of small Bracken Clock beetles. They live chiefly amongst the fern. Many of them find their way into the water where the fish are watching for them. A trout usually makes a splashy rise at one of these beetles.

The largest, and therefore the most nourishing, item on the trout's menu is undoubtedly the stonefly, then come shrimps, and caddis, plus the beetles above mentioned. Larvæ and nymphs of many other smaller insects are also taken. As the size and weight of the fish depend upon the commisariat department, the more you can increase the items which appeal to the trout, the better. Pools made by damming the beck add greatly to your sport, because the fish are soon attracted to them, and as you work your way upstream you get rise after rise, where previously there was little or nothing doing. It is then you reap the reward of your labours.

Wherever the beck is bordered by trees and undergrowth, you will find other work to which you can turn your hand. Winter floods may alter the course of the stream, particularly at a bend, by undermining the bank, and a subsequent landslide probably brings down trees and bushes which ruin what was previously a fishable corner. As the seasons pass, certain reaches become overgrown, and the offending branches need cutting back. On some rivers the matter of shade is important because trout appreciate it, thus the trimming should not be too drastic. As far as a rocky beck is concerned, however, the fish can get plenty of shade under the banks and behind boulders, thus I should always trim sufficiently to enable you to cast a fly without the risk of getting hung up. Choose a time for doing the work when the water is low, for it is easier then, as you can wade practically anywhere, and the cut material can be removed without much interference from the current. If you have ever tried to manhandle a heavy branch against the pull of swift water, you'll know what I mean. Tools which you will find useful for the job include an axe, saw, bill-hook, flexible chain saw, and long-handled seccateurs. The chain saw comes into its own when you cannot reach over-hanging branches by other means. A rope is attached to each end of the saw. One rope is thrown over the branch, and the saw is then pulled into position. Two people are required to work it. When building dams or trimming the beck, you have to wade. Now a stony river bed affords most precarious foot-hold, unless you wear waders with leather soles and plenty of hobnails. Hip-length rubber boots with rubber barred soles are anathema, for they slip at every step, and most of the time your heart is in your mouth. Hobnails are the only thing that will prevent you slipping when you are working in the beck, or fishing it. The feeling that you can't keep your feet, takes most of the pleasure out of a day's fishing on a rocky stream.

When in flood, water is an extraordinary powerful medium, and causes very considerable erosion where the current can work its will. It is usually at an unprotected bend that the greatest damage is done. On a beck which I often fish, the water flows round a bend at the foot of a high steep face before disappearing into a rocky gorge. Between thirty and forty years ago the bend was protected by a wall, but this stone facing slowly disintegrated until little or nothing was left. At that time a cart track crossed the face of the slope, on which scattered larches and other trees grew. Now the track has gone, and with it many of the trees, leaving others in precarious positions. Below the face there is a long run that usually holds trout, but when you are fishing it you have to keep your eyes open lest an avalanche of wet soil falls and traps you. Had the stone facing been repaired when it first showed signs of wear, the hill face would have been saved, and with it the cart track and the trees.

Besides affording shade, overhanging trees supply a considerable amount of trout food in one way and another. A season or two ago we had a perfect plague of caterpillars in Lakeland. They hung in festoons on the trees, from which numbers of them fell into the beck where they were greedily devoured by the fish. Where cress, marsh marigolds, etc., grow at some distance from the beck, you can help the passage of trout food to the main stream in the same way that you present the trout with a welcome feed of tadpoles, *viz.*, by cutting small channels in the swampy ground so as to allow the water to trickle away at a faster rate, and carry with it various items on the menu. When not actually fishing, there is always something to be done on the hill-stream that will help to improve your sport. Should a drought come, then is your chance to build your dams or strengthen those already constructed if they show signs of wear and tear. Trees and bushes can be trimmed, and water thus kept open for fly-fishing which would otherwise be hopelessly grown up.

CHAPTER X

A WORD ABOUT RODS

IN a previous chapter I have said that proper presentation of your fly or flies is all important. The man who can present his fly seductively scores heavily over the angler who is less adept. To throw your fly you require a rod, and the latter is therefore the most important item of your outfit.

Rods, even when made to the same pattern, are never exactly alike, nor do two anglers handle their rods in a precisely similar manner. You need a rod, therefore, that suits your own particular style, so that brain, arm and rod work in unison without conscious effort. No matter whether you buy a greenheart or a split bamboo—the latter for preference—get the best you can afford. A first-class split bamboo will last you your lifetime if you look after it.

BALANCE OF A ROD.

The most important thing about a fly-rod is balance. No matter how good the material and workmanship may be, if the balance is wrong it will never throw a fly properly. I stress this matter of balance, because in the course of a long experience, I have met numbers of brother anglers by the waterside who seemed quite content to ply their craft with weapons that were to say the least of it, ill-balanced. Again and again when in conversation with such anglers have I "hefted" their rods, and made some polite remark when they asked me what I thought of them. You can't very well tell a complete stranger that his rod is point-heavy, yet the majority of rods are. It is easy to say that a rod can be balanced by a reel of suitable weight, but nowadays reels are so often made of aluminium alloy that they weigh practically nothing. Personally I should like to see rods balanced, or in other words show no sign of point-heaviness, when they leave the builders. Later, when a reel is attached such a rod will still balance well, because the extra weight is all " in the hand " where it is not felt. So long as the weight is in the butt, it takes a great deal of it before it inconveniences the angler.

The mention of the word " weight " is abhorrent to many anglers, and they may perhaps be forgiven for showing such abhorrence, seeing that the weight in the majority of rods is badly distributed. The difference in weight between a 9 ft. rod of 12 oz. and a similar weapon of 4 oz. will make the average angler choose the latter, but if the weight in the 12 oz. weapon is in the right place it will handle as sweetly, and the weight will be no more felt during the course of a day's fishing, than would be the case if the 4 oz. rod was used and its balance was untrue.

Many years ago I sent for a fly-rod, and when

it arrived I put it together, attached a reel, and made a few trial casts on the lawn. Ten seconds was sufficient to tell me that the weapon was badly balanced, being almost as point-heavy as a clothes-prop. As the weight of the aluminium alloy reel was practially negligible, something had to be done to make the rod efficient. Barring its evil balance it was and still is an excellent weapon, and has accounted for some heavy trout. Without going into details, I may say that I corrected the balance by adding lead to the butt, and when the rod was ready for action it weighed in the neighbourhood of 12 oz. On subsequent occasions when meeting anglers by the river, they showed surprise at and admiration for the balance and ease with which this rod could be manipulated.

PRESENTATION.

When buying a certain pattern of rod, it is well to try a number of that pattern until you hit upon one that suits your style and action. Given a well-balanced rod, a tapered line, and a tapered cast, it is then up to you to present your fly attractively.

Some men have an uncanny knack with a fly-rod, but practice generally enables the average angler to present his fly with delicacy and precision.

The weight of the line should be in proportion to the power of the rod. A too-light line is quite as bad as one that is too heavy. The novice who chooses a line for wet fly-fishing generally errs on the light side.

As a man grows older his eyesight doesn't improve, and a line of a colour that he can easily see is a great help. Lines of a green shade are difficult to see, whereas a yellow-dressed line shows up well, especially on a dark day.

With regard to reels, I can never understand why the makers always place the handle on the right side. Most of us are right-handed by nature, yet the minute we hook a fish we are supposed to transfer the rod to the left hand, and reel in with the right. Why change hands at all? It seems to me that a left-handed reel is more sensible. Rod manipulation is natural to the right hand, while the left falls instinctively on the reel handle. In the case of a fixed spool reel the handle is on the left side, yet men use it quite naturally, despite the fact that the handles of their fly-reels are on the right.

Professional tackle-makers invariably varnish their rods so that they have a glossy surface. This is ostensibly done to protect the weapons from wet. As a measure of protection varnish is excellent, but on a sunny day the light from it flashes like a heliograph and alarms the trout. Far better paint your rod with a matt surface in some neutral shade like heron-grey.

To-day the supremacy of the split-bamboo fly rod is threatened by the tubular steel rod. More than forty years ago I first used tubular steel fly and bait rods in Canada. While the steel fly-rods of that day were more or less of a washout as regards their balance and action, the short bait-casting rods did their work quite well. With one of these rods I killed a lot of black bass, both small-mouth and large-mouth, as well as pickerel, perch, etc. For rough trips in the woods a steel spinning rod proved handy enough, as it was practically unbreakable.

Since then, American steel rods have been greatly improved, and certain manufacturers on this side of the Atlantic have taken them up, and are turning out some really first-rate weapons. The modern English-made steel fly-rod will cast a fly quite as well as a split bamboo or a greenheart. They have two decided advantages over cane or wooden rods, inasmuch as they are practically unbreakable, and quite unaffected by weather conditions. Combining lightness with power, they are also very quick, and so extremely certain in hooking. To get the best all-round results with a steel fly-rod, the line should be rather heavier than for a split-bamboo or wooden rod of the same proportions, as the trajectory with the steel rod is higher. Using a single-handed steel trout rod you can kill a salmon in shorter time and with greater ease than is the case with a long, double-handed split-bamboo or wooden rod. Excellent steel spinning rods are also on the market, and that these rods have come to stay is undoubted.

A SELECTION OF GOOD FLIES

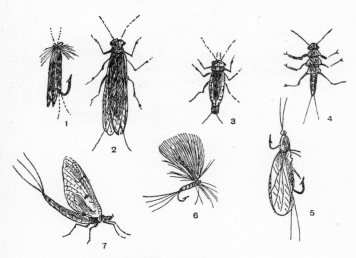

1. ARTIFICIAL STONEFLY
2. FEMALE STONEFLY
3. MALE STONEFLY (JACK)
4. CREEPER
5. NATURAL-ARTIFICIAL STONEFLY
6. ARTIFICIAL GREEN DRAKE
7. GREEN DRAKE

See pages 65, 66 and 68

KNOTS FOR ATTACHING LINE
TO SWIVEL ON TRACE

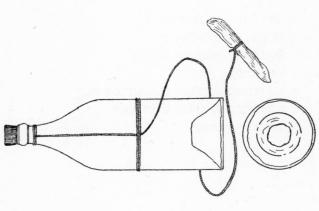

HOME-MADE GLASS BOTTLE
MINNOW TRAP

See page 52